Lone Girl Flyer

Anthony Masters

Illustrated by Linda Clark

an imprint of Hodder Children's Books

Amy Johnson (1903-1941)

1 July 1903 Amy Johnson was born in Hull. After school, she studied at Sheffield University.

15 September 1928 Amy had her first flying lesson with the London Aeroplane Club.

1929 Amy flew her first solo flight on 9 June, and on 10 December she became only the second woman to obtain her ground engineer's licence.

1930 On New Year's Day, Amy declared that she intended to break Hinkler's 1928 record for solo flight to Australia. She left Croydon Aerodrome on 5 May, landed in Australia on 24 May, and was awarded the CBE on 3 June. The plane she flew can be seen today in the aviation display at the Science Museum in London.

29 July 1932 Amy married Jim Mollison, also a long-distance flyer.

1936 Amy broke the previous record for solo flight from London to Cape Town.

1939 After divorcing Jim Mollison, Amy joined an independent air transport company. When war broke out, the company was taken over by the Air Ministry.

1940 On 20 May Amy joined the Air Transport Auxiliary as a Second Officer. She wrote her last letter to her parents on 29 December.

5 January 1941 Amy's plane crashed in the Thames Estuary. She is thought to have parachuted out but then been hit by a ship and drowned.

Chapter 1
Tom's Lucky Day

'I've got a surprise for you,' said Mrs Charlton to her twelve-year-old son, Tom. 'Something's happened at work.'

Tom's mother was secretary to Lord Wakefield, a wealthy oil tycoon with an interest in flying.

'Lord Wakefield's decided to sponsor Amy Johnson's solo flight to Australia and he wondered if you'd like to meet her.'

Tom could hardly believe his luck. He'd always dreamed of becoming a pilot. Now he was going to meet someone whose dream had come true.

Flying had become fashionable in the 1930s. The Moth, nicknamed 'the motor-car of the air', was a sturdy and practical light aeroplane designed by Geoffrey de Havilland. By 1928, Moths had been exhibited in several London department stores. Everyone believed flying had an exciting future, but at the moment this was a sport for rich people, and almost half the light aircraft in existence were privately owned.

From the perimeter of the airfield at the flying school, Tom and Lord Wakefield watched Miss Johnson practising for her flight. She already knew how sensitive the controls of a Moth could be. The slightest pull on the control column put her into a climb. The slightest finger push forward and the plane began to dive.

'How long does it take to go solo?' asked Tom.

'The average time is about ten to twelve hours,' said Lord Wakefield. 'But Amy's taken fifteen hours and forty-five minutes. Of course she had to save up for the lessons and that made far too many gaps between them.' Lord Wakefield paused before admitting, 'Amy can be rather heavy-handed with the controls. She often has a problem making a smooth landing.'

Tom watched tensely as Amy landed. Sure enough, she came down too fast and the Moth slewed round on the runway, just missing a couple of oil drums.

'She's more of an arriver than a lander,' said Lord Wakefield.

'Does that mean she's no good?' Tom asked anxiously.

'It just means she hasn't got natural co-ordination. But we reckon Amy makes up for that with her determination.'

A few minutes later, Amy strode past them towards the hangar, looking furious. When she saw Lord Wakefield she yelled, 'Sorry about that. Bit of a bumpy landing.'

'At least you missed the oil drums,' he replied.

Then Amy caught sight of Tom. 'Who are you then?' she asked abruptly.

'Hello Miss Johnson. I'm Tom Charlton. I want to be a pilot too.'

Amy's mood seemed to lighten. 'It's not easy. You can see that,' she said with a grin. Then she added warmly, 'And you can call me Amy.'

'I'm going to follow your route,' Tom said eagerly. 'I've mapped it out in the attic.'

Amy was moved. 'Thanks,' she said. 'I don't have a team to back me up, you know. This is a solo flight in every sense of the word. It'll be good to know you're thinking about me.'

Amy was due to begin her flight to Australia from Croydon Aerodrome, South London, on 5 May 1930. Tom and his parents were staying the night at a nearby hotel.

In the early hours, unable to sleep for excitement, he wandered into the deserted lounge.

To his surprise, Amy was gazing out of the window. She looked tired and frail, but she grinned at Tom when she recognized him. 'I've got a pounding headache – but everyone thinks I'm going to fly to Australia this morning, so I suppose I'll have to.'

'Are you afraid?' asked Tom hesitantly.

'Flying's my life,' she replied. 'I can't afford to be afraid. Neither will you when your time comes.'

They shook hands.

'I'll be with you all the way,' he promised.

Amy smiled at him gratefully.

Chapter 2
Amy Begins Her Journey

The morning was cold when Amy's Gipsy Moth *Jason* was wheeled on to the runway. Tom watched the preparations for her departure in an agony of nerves. Supposing something went wrong? The Moth looked incredibly small and fragile, and so did Amy. A few photographers had turned up to take pictures, and she posed in a fur-collared Sidcot suit, goggles draped over her flying jacket.

Amy was determined to beat the previous record-holder, Bert Hinkler. Last year he had been the first pilot to complete the 11,000 mile solo flight to Australia.

Soon everything seemed ready for take-off. But at the last minute Amy noticed a strong smell of petrol and discovered a dripping pipe connector.

Fortunately the Croydon mechanics were able to mend the leak without having to drain off the tanks. But Tom felt this was a bad start. So did Amy.

Eventually, at about half-past seven, Amy clambered back into her cockpit and then paused to give Tom a wave. He waved back, thrilled that she had remembered him.

Amy had never taken off with such a
heavily over-loaded aircraft before. It had
three petrol tanks (more than four times
that of a normal Moth) and a selection of
heavy tools and spares. Amy knew that, to
get *Jason* off the ground, she would have
to push the joystick forward at the very
beginning of her take-off run. If she didn't,
there would be no time to throttle back
and she would hit the boundary fence.

Tom watched tensely as Amy taxied

down the grass runway as fast as she could.

As the Moth sped along, one of her
mechanics cupped his hands and yelled,
'Get your tail up!'

Amy came to a halt just before the fence.
Later, as she tried to take off again, she
shouted, 'I'll take off how I choose – and
get out of the way all of you!' Then she
caught sight of Tom and gave him another
wave and a thumbs-up sign.

For the second time Amy taxied down-
wind, turned and opened up the throttle.
As *Jason*'s tail came gently up, the Moth
cleared the fence and began to climb.

By late afternoon, Amy had landed at Aspern Aerodrome near Vienna in Austria, and the next day she flew from Vienna to the Turkish city of Istanbul.

The normal cruising speed for Moths was 90 miles per hour, but *Jason* had been fitted with a heavy airscrew and flew rather more slowly.

Amy had also experienced further trouble from the leaking petrol pump and was forced to do all her own pumping 'with my face over the side of the ship'. This meant that at each stroke a jet of petrol spurted into the cockpit.

Amy had planned to land an hour before sunset. In spite of being buffeted and soaked by rain, she landed at San Stefano in Turkey with an hour to spare.

Back in his attic, Tom was setting up
Amy's stopovers on his model flight path,
writing the names of the airports on
miniature flags. He had worked out that
tomorrow Amy would have to cross the
Taurus Mountains and wondered how she
was feeling, alone in such a small aircraft.

Chapter 3
High Winds
and Sandstorms

Amy was just as nervous as Tom had imagined as she tried to climb above the cloud layer that hid the peaks of the Taurus. Later, she recorded the hazards in her log:

'I climbed steadily to 8,000 feet, then 10,000 ... and then more slowly to 11,000. At this height my engine started an ominous coughing and spitting and I realized that I couldn't go any higher.'

Amy descended to 10,000 feet and tried to follow the railway line through the winding gorges.

'I had one very unpleasant moment when threading my way through an exceptionally narrow gorge, with the mountains rising sheer on either side of me only a few feet from my wings and towering high above. Rounding a corner I ran straight into a bank of low clouds and for an awful moment could see nothing at all.'

In desperation she tried to dive below the clouds, emerging at a speed of 120 miles per hour, with one wing down, aiming straight for a wall of rock. She just managed to straighten *Jason* up in time, but was badly shaken.

At dawn the next morning she left Aleppo for Baghdad in Iraq.

Later that afternoon, Amy was flying at 7,000 feet to avoid bumpy weather.

A heat haze was already making visibility poor, but much thicker cloud loomed ahead. Suddenly the Moth gave a tremendous lurch, the nose dipped and *Jason* plunged down a couple of thousand feet.

Amy struggled with the controls, but sand and dust had covered her goggles. Then, to her horror, she felt the wheels touch the ground.

Hurriedly, Amy switched off the engine and got out, trying to turn *Jason* round to face the wind. But the force of the gale pushed the Moth backwards. Panicking, she grabbed all her luggage from the cockpit and placed the suitcases behind the wheels.

Amy's next job was to keep the dust and sand out of the carburettor over which she finally managed to fasten a canvas cover. Then she climbed on top of the engine and tied a hanky over the air-vent hole in the petrol tank.

Turning her back to the wind, Amy sat on *Jason*'s tail to anchor the plane while she waited for the storm to blow itself out.

Amy later wrote in her log: 'After about three hours the wind began to die down, so I picked up my luggage, swung the propeller and took off in the direction I thought Baghdad would be in.'

Chapter 4
A Bumpy Landing

Amy made a bad landing at Baghdad and
Jason swung round, snapping an undercarriage strut. Unless repairs could be made
fast she would have no chance of breaking
Hinkler's record. She remembered how she
had nearly made the same mistake at flying
school – when Tom had been watching.

Amy had often thought about her young
supporter during her flight. There was
something about Tom's enthusiasm for
her great adventure that made Amy feel
less alone.

'*Jason*'s damaged,' Mrs Charlton told Tom. 'But Lord Wakefield's sure she'll still break the record. In fact he made a bet with me.'

'How much?' asked Tom eagerly.

'A pound.'

'I'll bet you sixpence, Mum,' said Tom. 'It's all I've got.' In fact he was desperately worried about Amy, now that he was starting to realize just how demanding her flight was. Was she going to survive? He so wanted to see her again, safe and well.

Thanks to the Manager of Imperial Airways at Baghdad, the broken strut was replaced at a nearby air force base.

Next morning Amy took off, with the engine overhauled and the new strut in place.

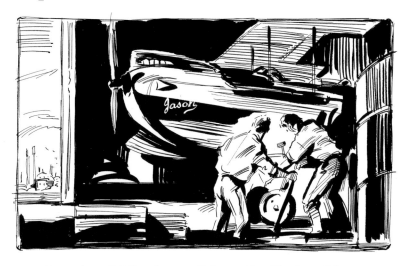

On the fifth day of Amy's flight, Tom picked up the morning paper and saw the headline 'LONE GIRL FLYER'. He felt a rush of emotion. Would he ever see a similar headline about himself? Like, 'LONE BOY FLYER'? Perhaps…

While travelling to the Persian Gulf on 9 May 1930, Amy wrote in her log: 'Circling round and round in the bumpy air I searched for an aerodrome. Finding none, I became anxious and looked round for a space large and flat enough to land.'

At last she found somewhere, but the ground was uneven and she sheared a bolt securing the top of the new strut.

Fortunately, help was at hand again.

This time some local British officials arranged for repairs to be made. Amy was soon heading for Karachi, still with a chance of breaking the Hinkler England-India record.

'You're going to lose your bet, Mum,' Tom said excitedly as he wrote the name 'Karachi' on one of his flags.

'It's going to be a close thing,' Mrs Charlton admitted, smiling.

Despite engine trouble, Amy looked as
if she was going to win Tom's bet for him.
Hinkler had reached India on the eighth
day of his flight. She arrived on the sixth.

Tom's heart almost burst with pride
when he saw the newspaper headline:
'THE BRITISH GIRL LINDBERGH'. Charles
Lindbergh, another one of his heroes, had
flown the Atlantic on 20 May 1927.

Now Amy was being treated as a real
celebrity and Mrs Charlton told her son,
'Lord Wakefield's delighted.'

Chapter 5
More Setbacks

Allahabad was to be Amy's next stop, but she had difficulty in identifying it from the air and landed at Jhansi to ask directions. Later she recorded in her log: 'After an hour's flying, the petrol from my second reserve tank gave out and I saw from the gauge on my remaining tank that I only had sufficient petrol for another hour's flying.'

Amy realized she must have had strong head-winds and turned *Jason* round, knowing she was not going to be able to make Allahabad without refuelling. She returned to Jhansi, but made yet another bad landing, causing more damage.

When Tom heard about Amy's latest disaster, his fears for her increased. That night he dreamed of her, looking incredibly young, with an ill-fitting pair of khaki shorts and a flying helmet. The skin on her face, arms and legs was burnt and blistered by the sun, and tears were not far from her hot, tired eyes. Half awake, Tom saw her plane falling from the skies, turning in circles until it hit the desert floor. He woke up in tears, and then felt a surge of relief as he realized he'd only been dreaming.

After crossing the Ganges Delta in her much-repaired Moth, Amy followed the coastline towards Burma. But more problems soon faced her. She became lost over the mountains in blinding rain, eventually making a crash landing in a playing field at Insein, 5 miles to the north of Rangoon.

Jason now had a smashed propeller, a ripped tyre, a broken undercarriage strut and a badly damaged wing.

When Tom heard what had happened he was sure Amy wouldn't be able to continue. He had lost his bet. But that wasn't important. It was Amy's survival that really mattered.

Meanwhile, Amy was writing in her log: 'I was quite unable to cope with the situation that night and begged to be allowed to go to bed at once.'

But her luck held out. By an amazing coincidence she had crash-landed near a government technical college whose students worked through the night to make *Jason* airworthy again.

Next morning, refreshed by a long sleep, Amy fitted a new propeller and cleaned up the mud-caked engine.

But she knew she had lost her lead over Hinkler and was deeply depressed.

Tom could still think of nothing but Amy's flight and his school friends were always teasing him about her.

'This Amy Johnson – didn't you meet her at Croydon Aerodrome?' asked Brian.

'I did happen to see her off,' Tom replied casually.

'So you must have taken a real fancy to her then?' asked Jack, and Tom rushed at them both, fists flying.

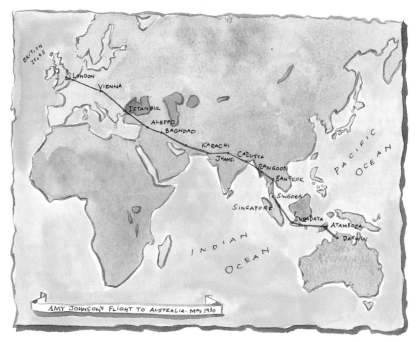

AMY JOHNSON'S FLIGHT TO AUSTRALIA. MAY 1930

Chapter 6
A Telegram for Tom

On the morning of Monday 19 May, Amy left Singapore for Surabaya in the Dutch East Indies, but ran into bad weather over the Java Sea.

'The wind began to blow and the waves rose ... the clouds got thicker and the rain fierce ... it was equally black in every direction ... I circled round and round ... I knew that thousands of hungry sharks were waiting.'

On Thursday 22 May, Amy put down at Timor but wasn't able to telephone the nearest British official to say she had landed safely. As a result, on Friday 23 May, the headlines read: 'FLYING GIRL MISSING'.

Tom was horrified. He couldn't believe that, after all the dangers she had faced, Amy had been killed.

On Saturday 24 May, Tom had still heard nothing and was in despair. Then the bell rang and he raced downstairs to find a messenger boy at the door.

'Lord Wakefield's compliments,' he said. 'This telegram's for you.'

Ripping open the telegram with trembling hands, he read:

'TOM. SAFE AND WELL IN DARWIN. NOT EVEN A BUMPY LANDING WHICH MAKES A CHANGE. SEE YOU IN ENGLAND. LOVE, AMY.'

Stanley Baldwin, the British Prime
Minister, sent a telegram to Amy's father:
'PLEASE ACCEPT MY WARMEST
CONGRATULATIONS ON YOUR DAUGHTER'S
WONDERFUL ACHIEVEMENT WHICH HAS
STIRRED THE IMAGINATION OF ALL BRITISH
PEOPLE THROUGHOUT THE EMPIRE.'

Tom certainly had every reason to be proud of his lone flyer.

Amy Johnson had begun her flight to Australia as a relatively inexperienced pilot. She had never even flown outside the United Kingdom before. But when she returned they needed special barricades to hold back the crowds at Croydon Aerodrome.

Dusk had fallen as Tom watched Amy's slight figure clamber on to a hastily erected platform lit by a beacon normally used for night landings.

She had not only proved that a woman could succeed in what had been largely a male world, but she had put the De Havilland Moth through extensive testing. Although Amy had failed to beat Hinkler's record, she was awarded a CBE for her pioneering flight.

Amy gave a short speech, followed by applause from the onlookers.

As she began to push her way down through the crowd, Tom thought he should make himself scarce. Amy wouldn't want to talk to him when she was so busy.

Instead, spotting him, Amy Johnson ran up to Tom and shook his hand.

'Thanks.'

'What for?' Tom asked in bewilderment.

'Believing in me,' she said.

Glossary

airscrew the propeller of a plane

carburettor apparatus for mixing fuel with air, to convert into vapour, for running an engine

CBE Commander of the British Empire; a medal given for a special achievement

down-wind moving with the wind

goggles protective glasses

head-winds winds blowing against the front of a plane

joystick the control lever used by the pilot of a plane

log the official record of a plane's progress; filled in by the pilot

Sidcot suit all-in-one protective flying suit

taxi when a plane runs along the ground under its own power

shear cut off

undercarriage strut a rod that supports a plane's landing gear